Pocket Monologues for Men

Pocket Monologues for Men

Edited by

Roger Karshner

Dramaline Publications
36-851 Palm View Road, Rancho Mirage, CA 92270

Library of Congress Cataloging-in-Publication Data

Pocket Monologues for men/edited by Roger Karshner.
        p.   cm.
    ISBN 0-940669-41-2
    1. Acting. 2. Monologues. I. Karshner, Roger.
PN2080.P63   1998
808.82'45'081—dc21   98-22435

Cover art by John Sabel

CONTENTS

RURAL

EUGENE LINN SHAW

Eugene Linn's sadness was deep in him after his father died. Here Eugene delivers a poignant speech regarding his feeling for his recently departed dad.

EUGENE LINN SHAW

Everyone says, "Ya gotta git ahead, ya gotta git ahead." Why, hell, seems like that's all I ever hear anymore. "Ya gotta git ahead." Hell, what is a man, anyway? Just a big ole gittin'-ahead machine, a big buncha nothin' pushin' 'is life through a keyhole? Besides, what's gittin' ahead have t' do with anything, anyhow? Heck, my dad was a man. Yer damn right, 'e was. He was really somethin'. He was a real pisser, that guy, a real cut off the ole plug. Why, he never cared nothin' 'bout gittin' ahead. I don't mean 'e was lazy er nothin' like that, he jus' didn't give a dern fer nobody. He didn't give a hoot if school kept er not. He was his own man, my dad. An' 'e was tougher'n a pine knot, too, that ole devil. Could outwork three men an' a boy. Was a-workin' right up till the day 'e died. He was a good man. An' 'e had a smile bigger'n Ross County.

I sure loved that old man. I loved 'im more'n anything. But I never told 'im so. Damn! I wished

I'da told 'im. But 'e always seemed too big and too busy. But I sure loved 'im, all right. An' 'e loved me, too. Derned right, 'e did. He never ever told me so, but I could tell. You kin feel them things. I sure wish I'da told 'im how I felt about 'im. Damn!

(*He looks upward as though looking through the ceiling. His voice rises plaintively as he attempts to reach beyond the grave.*) I love ya, Dad! Do ya hear me? I love ya, Dad! I love ya, old man! I love ya, ya old shitkicker! Ya old pisser! Do ya hear me? You were a big man, old man, a helluva man! An' I love ya, Dad, I love ya!

DOYLE RUCH

Doyle Ruch has a smile that busts out often, all over his face. He loves farming but is saddled with a city job, a success-oriented wife, and unappreciative in-laws who lean on him for support. When Doyle speaks of the land, of farming, his eyes buzz with delight, and that big unruly smile devours his face. Here he reflects on happier times:

DOYLE RUCH

On real cold mornin's, I usta harness up the team 'fore I led 'em down t' the pound fer a drink. I 'member the harness usta be all frozen an' stiff an' hard t' bend. M' hands usta git colder'n hell. Damn canvass gloves never did keep yer hands warm. By the time I got through a-bucklin' that frozen harness, m' hands'd be achin' an' numb.

The horses could feel the cold, too. They'd jus' stand there a-lookin' straight ahead with big frosty breaths a-comin' outta their snoots. Poor goddamned horses, they didn't wanna go noplace. You could tell what they was a-thinkin'. "Dumb sonofabitch. What the hell's 'e wanna go out in them fields t'day for? He oughtta be up at the house settin' in the kitchen where it's warm."

5

After I got the team harnessed, I usta lead 'em on down t' the pond behind the springhouse. I 'member how the wagon tracks an' the horses' hoof prints usta freeze over, an' ya had t' walk real careful fer feara fallin' on yer breakfast. The horseshit even froze up, too, an' lay in the road like big iron balls. It's a good thing, frozen horseshit, 'cause frozen horseshit don't stink.

When I got the horses t' the pond, I usta bust a hole in the ice so they could drink. After they'd finished drinkin', I'd lead 'em on back t' the barn an' hitch 'em up t' the ole green wagon. An' when they was hitched, I'd lead 'em on out to the fields t' load up the corn that'd been piled up next t' the shocks. I'd pull the wagon up next t' the piles an' then git down an' scoop up the corn inta the wagon. I'd scoop away till the cold didn't bother me no more. An' after I'd been a-scoopin' fer awhile, nothin' bothered me, nothin'. There was jus' me, them horses, the corn, an' the quiet.

JOE CLARK

Joe Clark runs a general store in a small farming community. He is a nice man and everybody speaks highly of him. But he's never married due to a tragedy that has left irrevocable scars, has never married because of the loss of "a purty little thing."

JOE CLARK

Yes sir, she was sure a purty little thing. Her name was Martha and she lived over near Kingston. She was somethin'. Purty ain't the word for 'er. In fact, I don't think there's a word-spinner on the face o' the earth who could describe her with justice. And she was nice an' sweet an' 'er skin was just as soft as a cow's ear, it was. An' she usta treat me just like the kinga the world; made me feel special. An' she sure wasn't out after me for my money, either, that's fer sure. Heck, I was workin' at the feed mill then, pullin' down nothin' but debts. M' clothes was patches on patches. I had me this old car that was all rusted out. I was in one heckuva shape. But she still loved me; she sure did, all right.

She usta come meet me every night after work at the mill. Every night, rain 'er shine, she never missed.

7

I can just see 'er now, comin' up the road with 'er long hair flyin', 'er heels a-kickin' up sparks on the asphalt. Then one night after work I seen her comin' just like as usual; a-comin' along the roadway a-smilin' and tossin' 'er head just like always. And then, God knows why she did it, she stepped out on the highway without lookin'; stepped right out in front of a high-ballin' semi, she did. The guy couldn't stop. Wasn't his fault. She didn't give 'im a chance. Killed 'er outright.

She sure was a purty little thing.

DUDE HENDERSON

Dude is noted for being a handyman par excellence who can, as the locals say, "do anything." But the thing he preferred doing more than anything else was hanging out at the local bar and guzzle beer, a beverage he ingests voluminously, while bullshitting with the boys. Here, Dude waxes poetic regarding his favorite libation:

DUDE HENDERSON

(*examining the bottle of beer in his hand as if it were the Hope diamond*) Beer. Beer. Why hell, beer's the best damned drink in the world. An' it's honest lookin', just like it tastes. (*admiring the brew*) Jus' look at it. Prettier'n a woman in a sweater without underwear. Yer damned tootin'.

Hell, I sure usta put away the beer in the ole days. Back when I could bite a pine knot out of a two-by-four. I usta really put 'er away. Damn right! Usta drink beer till m' bladder felt like a-bustin' an' m' belly swelled up like a toad's. Usta drink an' piss, piss an' drink. Drink one an' piss two. I usta piss streams a beer s' damn pure it shoulda been bottled back up an' drank all over again.

9

I 'member some nights me an' somea the other guys usta git about half tight an' hold pissin' contests t' see which onea us could let 'er fly the farthest. One time ole Vemont Pearson put 'er almost twenty foot.

An' sometimes in the wintertime a whole buncha us usta git all pissed up an' try an' write our names an' cuss words in the snow. I 'member one night around the holidays when Jerry Congrove had enough pee stored up in 'im t' write "Merry Christmas an' a Happy New Year." Looked real purty, too. An' 'e did it standin' in a second-story winda.

Beer! Nothin' like it. Nothin' at all. Best damn drink there was an' ever will be.

ESTIL GOOD

At one time Estil had been offered a sales position, but—like so many to whom opportunity is a threat— he vacillated and, as a consequence, became a slave to a two-bit eatery. Here he reflects upon what might have been:

ESTIL GOOD

One time I was gonna give up this here greaseball. Was gonna go on up t' Cleveland an' become a salesman. I coulda bin the hottest-shot salesman ever t' open up 'is catalog on the counters of America. I had it in me. I was a born peddler. (*He reflects, then goes off into a fantasy sales pitch.*)

"Hello there, Mr. Buyer, how ya bin? How's the weather bin? Lotsa rain? No kiddin'? Why, we ain't had hardly any rain up in New York this year. Just moderatin'." An' then he'd say, "New York, Estil? Why, I didn't know you was livin' up in New York. Lordy." An' then I'd say, "Oh yeah, I bin up there ever since they made me Vice President a the company way back last spring." And he'd say, "Vice President. I'll be derned. Boy, you're sure somethin', Estil. Tell ya what. Jus' go ahead an' write me up fer ever'thing in yer catalog, okay?" (*He reflects for a spell and then returns to reality.*)

But, what the heck, all that travlin', runnin' 'round all over the place. No way fer a man t' live. At least here I got me security, a warm bed ever' night. I coulda had the job, though, oh yeah, damned right I coulda. (*beat*) But I jus' couldn't seem t' break outta this here one-horse place. The life wasn't fer me, I guess. Lotsa fellas go fer that kind a life, though. They love runnin' 'round all over. One hotel after another. Livin' outta a suitcase. An' they make big money, too. An' women. . . . (*He reflects for a moment on all the beauties out there on "the road," then snaps back.*) But, they's a buncha dopes. I'll bet most of 'em would like t' have a stake in a nice little business like this here. (*a long reflection*) I often wonder, though. Often wonder what kind a salesman I woulda made. I bet I coulda cracked the big 'uns an' made me a bundle. Prob'ly coulda made me a fortune.

DORSEY MOHLER

Dorsey lives ascetically on a small farm up in Fox Hollow. A naturalist, he know the Latin name for every plant and tree in the county and is, despite the fact that he's virtually uneducated, well-schooled regarding ecological matters and boomingly vocal about the "damned fools who spit in the eye of nature."

DORSEY MOHLER

Ya know, there just ain't nothin' as good as workin' the land; nothin' quite as satisfyin' as comin' t' grips with nature.

Know what? When ya think about it, the land's a whole lot like a woman. Yep, like a woman. She's got a lotta moods, a lotta mystery, an' she's beautiful. Yeah, beautiful. Like when the sun comes bustin' up over 'er of a-morning makin' 'er nice and soft-like. Then she takes on a whole buncha gold jewelry an' begins a-glintin' over the new day. An' when it rains, when it rains she lays there real sad like with big puddlesa tears in 'er eyes. An' the snow, the snow turns 'er inta an ice cube and she don't want nothin' t' do with ya fer a while.

An' the land, just like a woman, can make ya love 'er, make ya mad as hell. An' I'll tell ya, it takes a real man t' go ahead an' love 'er with ever'thin' 'e's got in 'im when she's a-goin' through 'er moods. An' the land, jus' like a woman, ya gotta make love to real easy. An' then, after yer done, ya gotta let 'er rest up fer a while, let 'er take a little nap before the next go-'round. An' if ya treat 'er right, if ya give 'er respect, she'll never let ya down.

(*He reaches down and scoops up a handful of earth, examines it, smells it.*) Ya know, this here farmland under m' feet is the best. It's rich! Just like a great big hunka chocolate pie. The crops that come outta this parta the country is as fine as they is in the world. An' ya know why? Ya know why? 'Cause the farmers 'round here treat it right, that's why, like they do their women. They're gentle and don't abuse.

JOHN CRIDER

*John is a man of heavily starched shirts and highly
shined shoes. He looks like wax. He's dapper,
snappy, well-tailored. He is also the proprietor of a
shoe store, and he speaks often and passionately
about shoes and the shoe business. Shoes are his life.
He loves shoes. When he talks of insteps and vamps
and styles and hard-to-fit customers, his eyes widen
perceptively.*

JOHN CRIDER

A shoe tells you a whole lot about a person. It's a
regular road map t' their soul. You can figure out all
about a person by studyin' 'is feet. Take your narra
foot, for instance. A narra foot tells you a person has
artistic ways. They either write poetry or paint or play
a musical instrument, or something. I call these kinda
feet "restless feet." Because people with artistic ways
tend to be unsettled. Like Dana Slade. She was a
7AA with a quad heel. A foot on her like a banana. I
got her for an artistic type from the moment I slipped
a William Greene mule on her foot. I said to myself,
This here is one restless person. And I was sure

enough right on the money. She ran off with that advance man for Pathe Pictures. Show business.

Now your person with wide feet is a whole different story. Wide-feet people are solid like the foundation they're standing on. They are also slow and usually boring. Like Sam Cunningham. Here is your typical twelve 12EE. A solid citizen. Why, he's been an Elk for forty years. Nice fella. But the man's so slow he's two days behind yesterday. And he could bore the stink off a hog. I sat next to him at the last Elk's picnic, and 'e spent the whole time talking about Mammoth Cave, Kentucky. He had all the dimensions and all the stuff about how it was formed way back when men were monkeys. And he wonders why Doris left him. Your typical EE.

We gotta whole bunch o' new models coming in next month. Latest outta the northeast. Finest leather, and latest styles. I can't wait to get those babies in my store window. They won't last a week. Remember those two-tone oxfords I got in last spring? Why, I sold them so fast my shoehorn almost caught on fire. People love smart shoes. Shoes. They're necessary, practical, and a new pair makes a person feel like money in a fireproof safe.

ED ZISSLER

Ed is the drummer/leader of a small-time band. He's a spirited fellow and conducts his outfit with verve and panache. Here he amplifies upon music and his involvement with it.

ED ZISSLER

I first started out in music with the accordion—a Wurlitzer. It was black and had ivory bass buttons. My name, Eddie, was spelled out in silver sparkle along the side of the keyboard. When I played, the silver usta flash an darn near knock the eyes outta people. My big number was "Lady o' Spain," and I usta play it for thunder. I wore a white silk shirt with floppy sleeves. I guess ya might say I was flashy. But I never liked the accordion.

I saw my first drum set in the window of Summers an' Sons in Chillicothe. Summers an' Sons was the big-deal music store in the county, and they advertised on the side of barns with snappy stuff like, "Teach a Boy to Blow a Horn, and He'll Never Blow a Safe." Summers an' Sons was way ahead when it came to outdoor advertising. I knew right away that the drums were for me, so I talked Mom inta trading the Wurlitzer for an' old bass drum an' a beat-up snare. Was the best move I ever made.

In high school, I was the star of the marching band and even won a drummers' contest up in Columbus. My sticks moved so fast when I played one of the judges wondered why I didn't get splinters.

I woulda gone on t' the big time, but when my dad came down with cancer, I figured I'd better help out 'round the farm. But I kept on drumming, and eventually organized the Ross County Stompers. We play most all of the music jobs in the area.

I love music more'n anything. Show me a person who doesn't, and I'll show you one sad son-of-a-gun.

WORKING CLASS

EDDIE
(Truck Driver)

Eddie drives a semi, or a "large car" as the drivers call them. He travels the States, picking up loads and delivering. It's a grueling life—one that borders on the monastic—that requires skill and intelligence.

EDDIE

Trucking's a lonely business. You're out there some damned place or the other most of the time. Away from your home and your family. The thing that gets to you the most is the fatigue factor and the shear loneliness of the occupation.

I'm usually on the road by seven or eight every morning and sometimes I'll drive till midnight. On a good day I'll chalk up six or seven hundred miles. These are the days I don't get hung up with loading and unloading and tarping and untarping or taking care of repairs or sitting around waiting for the dispatcher to find me a load.

Being on the road means you live on the run like some motorized Gypsy. Most of the time I bed down in the back of the cab, and my meals consist mostly of burgers and coffee, lots of coffee. A driver can forget all about gourmet meals. We have a saying: A seven-course dinner for a truck driver is a can of chili and a six-pack.

I call my wife about three or four times a week. Sometimes, after ten hours of bad, wet, angry highway, the sound of your wife's voice is the only thing that keeps you from telling 'em to take the job and shove it.

I miss Laurie and the kids. Three of 'em. A boy and two girls. We've got a little farm—ten acres—just outside South Bend. I don't get to spend as much time as I'd like to there, and that's the thing that wears at me most.

I'm driving extra time to salt away a few bucks and get off the road. I see myself as a woodworker, and eventually I want to set up a little business back home and live a regular life like other people. I've been out here on the road for a helluva long time. Longer than I ever thought.

What scares me the most is, if I'm not careful, I'm not gonna just be some guy who's out here driving a truck, I'm gonna wind up being a truck driver.

DAN
(Plumber)

The world of drains and traps and commodes is certainly not one of glamor. But Dan finds it interesting, challenging, and extremely lucrative.

DAN

Here you are, at home on Christmas, in the middle of checking out your new set of golf clubs, and you get this panic call from a woman who has a toilet stopped up. Her voice has this little catch in it, and you can tell she's close to tears because she's got fourteen people in the house, including her mother-in-law, who don't have anywhere to get rid of Christmas dinner.

So, you drag out in the middle of a snowstorm and go to the house where there's a living room full of bloated-looking people. You have to open up the john, a job which, incidentally—in the interest of good taste—I won't describe in great detail. After an hour, with your head in a quagmire, you get the thing open to the relief of all concerned. Then everybody thanks you and slaps you on the back and shakes your hand like you're this savior, or something. For a couple of minutes there you're Albert Schweitzer. Then you hand them your bill, and alluva sudden you're the Grinch Who Stole Christmas.

Plumbing's a rough job and you get into all kinds a situations with all kinds of people at all hours. You have to be kind of like a pipe-wrench psychologist, you know. Like when you show up at someone's apartment at two o'clock on a cold morning and a bathtub's running over and the people downstairs are creaming and kids are crying and the husband and wife are at each other's throats, you've got chaos on your hands, brother, and you've got to know what to do. And you've got to know how to handle the human element.

There's a lot more to plumbing than threading pipe.

FLOYD
(Painter)

Floyd has learned that there is far more to his job than painting.

FLOYD

I contract jobs of all kinds—from five-hundred dollars to ten thousand.

The killers are the smaller jobs where you get involved directly with the clients. For example: Here you've got this little old lady who lives in this house that's wall-to-wall with stuff she calls heirlooms that is actually junk. But to her every piece is like the Crown Jewels, so she takes you on this grand tour, commenting on everything and giving you background and details. Of course, the reason she's telling me all this is so we'll be extra careful when we paint. Heaven forbid we nick a fifty-cent plaster of Paris doorstop. But I listen and nod. I mean, what the hell? To her all this stuff's important.

Most people are very picky and finicky when it comes to painting. They deliberate and consider and haggle like crazy. You'd think they were getting a third opinion on major surgery. And they change their

25

minds like crazy. I sometimes sit for hours with people while they deliberate and agonize over the color charts. And I've learned to never recommend. No way. Are you kidding? If you do and they don't like the result—big trouble. So, I just sit back and listen and nod. What's it to me if they want to go for puce walls and a magenta ceiling? Hey, if they wanna turn their place into Santa's Village, it's their own damned business.

Patience is one of the major requirements for being a painter. That and putting on this act like you're super-concerned. Of course, I figure all this in the price. It's part of my fee. And I don't come cheap. After all—good actors get paid big money?

JIM
(Auto Mechanic)

Jim, a prisoner to grease, has learned that a car is much more than a piece of machinery. It's human.

JIM

They bring 'em in here and it's like they're human, ya know. Like they've got hearts and lungs and brains instead of engines and transmissions. "She doesn't sound right, Jim," they'll say.

And I'll say, "How *does* she sound?"

And they'll say, "Ker-chunk-a-chunk-a-chank."

And I say, "Oh."

And they'll say, "Is that bad?"

And I say, "Well, not as bad as ker-plunk-a-plunk-a-clang." Then I pop the hood and look inside. Then I go, "Oh, ah."

And they go, "Ah, oh."

I go, "Hum."

And they go, "Um."

It's like this ritual, you know. But it's important because it makes 'em think their car's special and that you're super concerned and it puts their mind at ease.

The men are worse than the women because they think they know everything there is to know about automobiles. Of course, I never let on they're wrong—which they are about ninety-five percent of the time.

We repair mostly high-priced imports. But grease is still grease. The grease from a Mercedes is just as impossible to wash off as the grease from a rusted-out Pinto.

I've scrubbed with every solvent known to man. Still, imbedded grease stands out in every line like these little black rivers. Look. (*He displays his hands, palms up.*) Is this a fortuneteller's dream, or what?

I used to be very self-consious about my hands around women until I ran into one who didn't care. We were married last October. She's a transmission tschnician for Aamco.

JOE
(Dishwasher)

Joe, on the rebound from drink, finds dish-washing excellent therapy.

JOE

I've got the lowest job in the kitchen—cleaning up the plates. I have to scrub 'em and get 'em steam-cleaned and stacked and ready for the cooks. It's a tough, sweaty job but real important because if they're aren't any dishes, people don't eat, okay?

Even though it's the lowest job, it's good because it's something and because now I'm working and making my way instead of sitting in a gutter some-place with a bag full of cheap wine and no future. All I was was a rag-bag, no-hope, whiskey-brained hunk of nothing. Until I got this job I was a living dead-man with no place to die.

The guy who owns the place, Sam Weller, he got me up off the street and got me a decent meal and offered me work. He said he'd take a chance on me if I was willing to take care of business and get my head out of my ass and get off the juice. Sam's a tough guy, but at the same time he cares. And with him there's no bullshit. So, he put me here in the kitchen and I've been here over a year, and I haven't had a taste since last January.

I almost went off the wagon a couple of times, but I hung tough. I had to. I mean, hell, a person can't go disappointing a guy like Sam, now, can he? It just wouldn't be right. After all, he believed in me and he taught me a lesson. He taught me that honest work can make your life mean something. Sam gave me hope.

Hell, the man gave me a life.

BURNETT
(Cowboy)

Burnett dispels the idea that working the range is a glamor job.

BURNETT

It's a hard life out here, mister. And fer chickenshit money an' no benefits. You gotta love this kind a life t' put up with it; gotta love the freedom of not havin' t' deal with people on a reg'lar basis.

People have this here idee about cowboys, ya know. They git it from yer books and yer TV and yer movies, an' the like. Everone's got the idee all it is is a-savin' the ranch and blowin' holes in the rustlers an' screwin' the rancher's daughter. (*chuckles*)

There ain't nothin' glamorous 'bout bein' a cowboy. Hell no, there never was. That there shit's all outta celluloid, all part a the glamor image put out by the Hollywood motion-picture business. People have the notion that the cowboy won the West. Hell, the cowboy didn't win the fucking West, the railroads won the fucking West. They think he run out the fucking outlaws. Hell, he didn't run out the fucking outlaws, the fucking outlaws became fucking businessmen. They think he took carea the Indians. Hell, he didn't take carea the Indians, the fucking Army took carea the Indians. The cowboy didn't do nothing but work 'is butt off an' eat dust an' git saddle sores.

An' everone's Western crazy these days, too. Everybody's runnin' around wearin' Levis an' workshirts an' Western hats an' boots. The cowboy's big business t'day with the fashion set because they've been convinced that this here is the life. I'd laugh if I didn't think I'd puke. (*He chuckles at the thought of it.*)

I'd like to see these here Polo and Guess Jeans cowboys and cowgirls out here in their thousand-dollar alligators an' designer pants. Hell, 'bout the first zero, bone-cold mornin' they had to roll out into a pile a steer shit, they'd be back to their BMWs in no time.

CLARENCE
(Mail Carrier)

Clarence, on the same route ("swing" as referred to by postman) for years, has keen perception relative to his occupation.

CLARENCE

I've been carrying mail on this route for nearly ten years. And neither storm and rain and snow and hail—nothing—has deterred me once from making my appointed rounds.

People are downright nuts, fanatics when it comes to their mail. Like it's the most important thing in their lives, you know. I guess this says a whole lot about the human condition because most of the time all they ever receive is crap.

After all of these years, I know most of the people on my swing intimately. It's like I've become part of their family. In some cases, in fact, I *am* family.

Like this one little old woman over on Maple Street, Mrs. Cartmell. Sometimes I think I'm the only friend she has on the planet. Her kids never come to see her—nobody. Only me, Clarence Withers, U. S. Postal Service carrier number ten twenty-five. She looks forward to me coming every day and always has coffee for me, or iced tea, or something like that. The other day she baked cinnamon rolls. I always spend a few minutes with her and listen to her problems. Hell . . . it's the least I can do.

At Christmas time I usually get a gift here and there. Cookies, candy, ties, cash. Cash is always welcome. Green goes well with everything. Mrs. Jamison, over on Whipple Avenue, she gave me fifty bucks last year. A hot-looking number down on Elm Street wanted to give me more than that—if you know what I mean. But I don't make those kinds of deliveries.

I guess some women just can't resist a man in uniform.

STAN
(Farmer)

Stan reflects upon farm life, his father, tradition.

STAN

I come down here every evening after the work is done. To be alone and reflect on the land. It's my way of paying respects.

It was my father who taught me to respect the land. In fact, he's the one who got me into the habit of coming down here like this. He used to come every evening, regardless of the weather, no matter what.

I can see him now: standing here with his cap in his hands, squinting out over the fields.

I think to be a good farmer you have to have a love affair with the land. You have to have this feeling for it that connects you to it in a spiritual way.

My father was only an eighth-grade-educated man. He didn't have the advantage—an advantage I received because of him—of an education. But maybe . . . maybe in some ways, he was the one who had an advantage because he *wasn't* schooled. Sometimes, if you're not careful how you handle it, too much education can cloud real feelings, can dirty

35

up the pure waters. (*pause*) Yep, my dad definitely had an edge in the feeling department, all right.

Even though farming's a hard life, it's a good life. Good because there's this directness to it, this clean edge, this clarity.

When I stand here, when I look out over the fields and smell the earth, and feel the wind and the sun and the rain and all of the little big things that make nature special, I know I'm blessed, I know that farming is a special thing. And from here I can see the little cemetery up near the maple grove where Dad is buried—where he sleeps under the land he loved so much.

I'm proud to be a farmer. And I'm real proud to be his son.

CONTEMPORARY

BOOKER

Always a profligate, Booker's life has degenerated even further due to a massive inheritance. Here, in a alcohol/drug stupor, he rails against his ilk and expresses contempt for himself, the life he leads—life itself.

BOOKER

The fucked-up goddamn bastards who live out here steamroller you with dollars, run you down with their wealth. They stampede you with bank accounts and stocks and bonds. They run roughshod over people and leave them in their wake because they don't care about feelings, because there's all this old money clogging up their veins. And you're part of it and you live with it because it's security, because it's all you've ever known. It's easy to be a rich shit because it doesn't take any moral fiber. You live with it rather than wander off into uncertainty. And, besides, I like this life of sleeping till I have to take a piss and not working and being able to afford the best alcohol and drugs. What's not to like, right? Why would anyone not want to be in my shoes? Look at this fucking room. That's a Degas over there, an honest-to-god real, authentic Degas worth two million bucks on a bad day at Sotheby's. And it's nice to have hanging on your wall because you know you can always sell the son-of-a-bitch if you need the money for alimony.

I hate this fucking life. I hate my friends. I hate my mother, who's a face-lifted socialite whose kindest words to me in her life were, "You look nice in your uncle Max's tux." My dad . . . he died from cirrhosis ten years ago and left forty million dollars in trust. The money comes in every month and gets pissed away in a day. I piss it away. I piss my life away. I piss on life. Why? Because there's nothing in it I can't afford!

LESTER

He just can't believe his friend is considering the purchase of a Ford Crown Victoria.

LESTER

Here's the skinny: You buy the Range Rover not because it's a good deal or rides good or handles good. We all know it's a piece of shit that looks like a hatbox on stilts. We all know it's an overpriced turkey that rides like a flatbed wagon. But this isn't the question here. The question here it how you're going to look, right? The question here is the perception of prestige, how people will relate to you when you pull up in this glorified tractor. Especially the kind of women you're interested in; the ones with money who play tennis with guys who look like pussies and dress out of Banana Republic. To them a Range Rover says you're Jim Wellington III who wears Brioni suits and uses a fork like he's afraid of food. You're a man who's been around, a guy with class, a guy with permanent creases in his chinos. You're all of this and more because you slide up in an olive drab British cube.

And here you are talking about buying a Crown fucking Victoria. Why in the fuck would you wanna buy a Crown fucking Victoria? This is a car for retired couples who can't back up without running over their lawn, who look like burnt toast from spending the few days they got left on this Earth in a fucking golf cart. A Crown Vic is a hearse. And you're actually thinking of buying one of these goddamn things, giving it serious consideration because it has lots of *trunk space*. What the hell kind thinking is this? Who gives a fuck about trunk space? Nobody who's happening gives a shit about how much Samsonite they can cram into the back of their car. Besides, the Rover has space up the ass in the back. And it doesn't project the image that you're on your way to the Elk's picnic.

Think today Ralph. Think of the rich, beautiful, tall blonde sitting next to you in your Range Rover with a cheetah in her lap. You buy a Crown Vic . . . next to you will be overweight pig with a wart on her nose. Get real.

DALTON

Dalton is convinced that his friend is making a tragic mistake by not making up with his very attractive girlfriend; an act he is convinced will lead to a lonely, sex-starved existence. Here, with the confidence of a seer, he councils his buddy regarding the fine art of reconciliation.

DALTON

What you wanna do is go over to her house and fall down on her doorstep and beg her to forgive you because you've been a horrible fucking jerk for forgetting her birthday. You plead, you beg, you grovel. Because, if you don't, you lose something that most men would eat a mile of slime for—a woman who's built like a goddess. And, after all, she's right. Here you go and forget her birthday, for crisesakes. This is stupid. This is no good. What does this tell the woman? It tells her that you're an inconsiderate little prick who's only hanging around to see her nude on a regular basis. Not that this is not an admirable, normal, reasonable thing. With all due respect, and I certainly don't mean any offense here, I'd give a good month's commission to see her in skin head to toe. What guy in his right mind wouldn't? But this isn't the point here. The point here is not blowing the opportunity for future visits to her bedroom. So you gotta make up with her. This is not even an option.

What you do is come up with a story. (*beat*) What? No! You can't do that! Telling her you just forgot isn't a story. It's a stupid admission of being an insensitive asshole. You tell her you forgot, you wind up in your bathroom with a back issue of *Penthouse*. You gotta have a story, a story that gets you off the hook and flatters her at the same time, okay? So you tell her you had to visit your mother's grave. (*beat*) So your mother's still alive, so what? She doesn't know that. Besides, your mother lives in Jersey, she may as well be dead. Anyway, you tell her that you had this tremendous grief because of your mother, who was a beautiful, feeling person—just like her. Okay? (*beat*) Of course it'll work. I've used it. It's foolproof. Not only will she understand, she'll be flattered by the comparison, and she'll hate herself for yelling at you. Here you'll have sympathy, flattery, and guilt all working for you in one neat little package. (*confidential*) And until you've had sympathy-flattery-guilt sex, my friend, you haven't lived.

GEORGE

*Doris's jealously has reached outrageous propor-
tions. She is even jealous of women in her dreams.
George's attempts to reason with her reveal another
quirky aspect of her personality—fractured logic.*

GEORGE

Doris, you can't do this. It's driving me bananas. Just
because you dream I'm having an affair doesn't mean
I actually am. This is not rational, Doris. This is sick.
Sick because it shows how damned insecure you are,
how goofed-up. It all has to do with your dad dump-
ing on you mother, running off with that ticket-taker.
I can understand this. If my old man had taken off
with a four-star bimbo, I guess I would be bent a little
emotionally, too. But you can't go carrying this stuff
around for the rest of your life. And it's seriously
fucking up our relationship. (*beat*) Why? Because
I'm really up to here with being accused of being
some kind of marauding animal. Hell, I'm not interested in anyone else. And now I'm catching hell for
having sex with some person in your dreams. You
don't think this is kinda over the edge?

What if I accused you of having sex with John Wilkes Booth? (*beat*) Yes, of course I know the man's dead. I read about it. The point I'm trying to make here is how irrational it would be. (*beat*) Was Booth handsome? Hell . . . I don't know. From the pictures I've seen I think he was kinda ugly. What the hell does this have to do with anything? (*beat*) You wouldn't have sex with an ugly man? I don't believe this. What I'm trying to do here is draw an analogy. (*beat*) So what if the girl in your dreams was beautiful, so what? (*beat*) It's okay for me to have sex with a beautiful woman but you have to have sex with a man's who's ugly. All right, all right! I'll change it. What if I dreamed you had sex with Cary Grant? (*beat*) Yes, or course I know his name was Archie Leach. So . . . ? (*beat*) No, I'm not suggesting you'd have sex with a man who wouldn't give his right name, I'm suggesting that it would be insane for me to accuse you of having sex with a person who's dead because it's an impossibility. (*beat*) You're not what kind of girl? (*beat*) One who would sleep with those kind of men. But you didn't sleep with them! Like I didn't sleep with the woman in your dreams. (*beat*) You have proof? How the hell can you prove something like that? (*beat*) Because I'm wearing the same watch. Doris . . . shut up and pass the toast.

BOBBY

Bobby and his older brother, Curtis, live in a land-locked area of North Dakota. Since the recent passing of their mother, the boys argue daily about Bobby's failure to accept her death He claims to see her glowing visage floating about the farm. Curtis, a brutish lout, berates and belittles him for this irrational behavior. Now, further complicating matters, Phil, their successful sibling, has come from the big city to wish them a happy Christmas. When Curtis, in an act typifying his hateful nature, denies him entrance, Bobby launches into the following tirade.

BOBBY

You never knew anything about her because you was always too wrapped up in your silly bullshit and hatefulness and fucking self. You was always turning away from her because you couldn't stand to have anybody give a shit for you, because down deep you know what a rotten bastard you really are. So don't go bad-mouthing her. You ain't got not right Curtis, no right at all. Keep your dirty remarks to yourself. She was an angel! She gave. She never cared about nothing but what was good for others. She had wings on her, that woman. Wings! She still does! I seen them last night when she was out front shimmering away like the Northern Lights do when they bounce over the snow sometimes. You think she's dead, but she isn't. Saints don't die. You resented her because she knew you and saw into you and knew you were a soulless shit. And you don't wanna help me. No way. You just wanna run my life, that's what. I'm just someone you need to have around to shove around and take out your meanness on. You're a nothing person. A big, empty, overgrown, mean, and contemptible asshole who gets off on seeing other people suffer and be afraid. Fear—that's your thing, Curtis, fear. Fear, because you're so goddamn afraid yourself. That's the thing that's got you. You know damn well what you are. Deep down you're a boatload of quivering Jell-O shit. Now let 'im in, dammit! He'll freeze to death out there! He's your brother, Curtis, your brother! Your flesh and blood, for God's sake! Just because he's successful, because he's something, you're scared shitless of him. Face it. Face up for once in your nothing, pissant life. I'm opening the door. If you wanna kill me, go ahead. I don't give a damn. Hell . . . I'm already dead.

MICHAEL

Michael delivers an impassioned speech regarding the dangers of total honesty.

MICHAEL

Hey, hey, just a minute here, now. I mean—that much honesty is stupid, okay? And besides, it's wrong. All of this business about spilling your guts, about getting everything out in the open, "telling it like it is," is bullshit—nonsense. Telling it like it is is usually an excuse for people to unload all their backed-up poison. Hey! Listen to me, here, okay? Are you listening?

Tell me what the hell ever happened to discretion and restraint? What the hell ever happened to respecting the feelings of others? Don't get me wrong, now. I don't mean we should go around lying all the time, but there are ways of laying the truth on people without loading it into a gun and blowing their brains out with it. Understand? Are you listening to me, here? Some people get heavy into therapy and that and then they run around with a goddamned couch on their back like psychiatric assholes. Know what I mean?

Okay, now, listen. Are you listening to me? The way I look at it, see, is that you can get said what you want without psychological diarrhea. And, besides, total honesty gets a lot of poor jerks into very big trouble. Like my dad had a thing going with our cleaning lady for years, okay? For years she came in every Monday to do the laundry and my old man. But you think my old man went blabbing to my mother, "Edith, every Monday while you're at the hospital rolling bandages, I'm rolling Marie"? Hey! My old man was no idiot. No way. He knew the importance of discretion, you know.

So, you gotta be careful how much you tell Ida. You go spilling the details about your ex-ladies, and you and Ida become history, okay? Then you're back to being a bachelor and playing with yourself and eating TV dinners. So, no matter how hard she pumps—pump, pump, pump—and they can pump, baby, they can pump. No matter how hard she pumps, you don't tell her shit, okay?

You're a virgin, remember? You're cherry. Are you listening to me here?

LARRY

Larry, an ex-jock, unashamedly reveals his homosexuality.

LARRY

Yes, that's right, Billy boy, you heard right—I'm gay. I came out over two years ago. The tendency was always there—underlying, you know. And it all came rushing forth when I met Rodney. We met in an antique shop where I noticed him staring at me over this lovely Early American quilt. There was an instant attraction.

This is the greatest thing that's ever happened to me. Now, finally, thank heavens, I'm comfortable with my sexuality. Now I'm finally over all the sports silliness: football and all that tackling and kicking and running and sweating and ugliness. Sports. Such a waste for a person with untapped creative talents.

Now I'm heavy into interior decoration. And I'm an absolute whiz, too. While I'm here I'll be happy to redo, if you like. (*observing the room critically*) Frankly, Billy, your place is rather drab. I suggest your earth tones: your browns, your soft greens, your golds, your russets, your basic autumn shades. And, oh yes—your bittersweets, definitely your bitter-sweets.

I'll say one thing for you, though, you keep the place neat as a pin. You must keep it covered with Saran wrap. But the furnishings? Oh my. Yuckie-wuckie, Billy boy, yuckie-wuckie. I suggest your moderns mixed tastefully with your antiques and your plants. Oh yes, your plants! Let them run wild, let them take over. Plants, plants, plants! I'm terrific with plants. I have quite a flair for casual greenery.

Rodney is *fabu*lous, you'll just love him. He's opened me up to so many things. My horizons are expanding like crazy. In heavy into Zen. With Shinto Goldberg. He was a rabbi who swung over. He's just *fabu*lous. You'll just love him. He's the author of *The Deli Way to Meditation*. It has to do with corned beef's influence upon Buddha.

Oh darling, this is going to be such a fun visit. I'm just dying to meet your fiancée. If you like her, she just has to be *fabu*lous.

RANDY

Why would any woman reject Randy? After all, he's such a "class guy."

RANDY

I musta asked her a hundred times. But every time she puts me down and makes me feel like shit. So, what the hell's the point? I mean, how many times can a dude get kicked in the balls by some broad, you know. These here California broads are a buncha goddamned snobs, man, a buncha assholes all trying to break into show biz. What's a regular guy like me gonna say to 'em? I mean, I don't know doodly shit about Shakespeare. I mean, what the fuck, man!

Last week, me and Eddie goes down to Palm Springs, okay? There was broads all over living hell down there, man. You've never seen so much ass in your life. And they hang out and drink and bullshit in these outfits that are like spray-painted on, you know. But like just try an' put a move on 'em. Hey, it's like you got B.O. or something, understand? I mean, c'mon!

I don't get it. I guess it's like Eddie says: "A lotta chicks today are fulla shit." And like Eddie knows from what's happening, man, 'cause this dude's been someplace, he's a hip guy. Like he says: "When you're dealing with broads with their heads up their asses, you ain't got a chance."

It's real hard to figure, you know. Maybe it's me. But hey! I mean like, after all, I ain't bad looking. And I been around. And I got bucks on me. I think it's just this ball-buster attitude that a lotta broads have nowadays. They get off on making a guy feel like he's wearing dirty shorts. It's no wonder alotta guys go for hookers. I mean, hey, a man's gotta have some release, you know. He's gotta get himself some self-respect somehow. I mean, how many times can a guy get shot outta the saddle by some slut who thinks her butt's made outta china?

It's real hard to figure. I guess broads these days just ain't interested in class guys like me.

LITTLE STICKS

Little Sticks speaks scathingly, admonishing his lis-
teners for living in the past, for not addressing the
present and facing the future. He touches on the
problem of alienation between parents and their chil-
dren.

LITTLE STICKS

Willya shut the fuck up about the goddamned drum
set? You talk like it's human, or something, like it
was everything in the whole world, for crisesakes. T'
hell with the drum set! What about Sticks? What
about him and what's happening today, right now,
and what he must be going through? What about his
feelings sitting there in the middle of a city dump
with half a mind? What about that? Fuck the set and
jazz and all of it. Screw the past and the so-called
good times that don't mean a crap to anybody or anything. Fuck yesterday and living between the pages of
a scrapbook with faded pictures that keep you from
facing up to what's going down now!

What about today? What about you, and what
about me, Harold "Little Sticks" Miller, the guy who
came in second to jazz and who's been living with his
head up his ass because he's been too bitter to for-

give? And what about Sticks? The poor bastard. Today he said something, he acted and talked to me through the drum set. It's the only way he could get things out of that World War III head of his; the way only a father could get into it about his son. Man, that's sad as hell. (*He turns, confronts Bobby, Birdie's father.*)

Like you. When are you going to get something going with Birdie? When are you going to quit talking shit and quit saying "wow" every other sentence and get down to it? When are you going to give her a chance and wake up to the fact that she ain't Charlie Parker? (*turning to Birdie*)

And you, you gotta knock off the crap, too, Birdie, and do what the hell you wanna do. Now, where the hell is Sticks? Exactly where the hell is he?

CLIFF

Cliff, a casualty of Vietnam, speaks bitterly of the war.

CLIFF

It was night, and we couldn't see a damned thing. They dropped a bunch of us up near the Mekong—from helicopters. Black as hell, it was, black as hell. We fell into mud up to our waists and some of the guys got stuck and couldn't move and were helpless and the Cong blew the piss out of 'em. You ever see anybody get blown away? Like forget it, man—it's the lowest.

Then all hell broke loose, like in the middle of a thunderstorm. The ground shook and puffs of fire lit up the fields like they were taking pictures with giant flashbulbs. I move off into this thick clump of trees and unhook my parachute and fold it up and Freddy and I —Freddy was my best buddy—then Freddy and I eased across a rice paddy toward Charlie, who was holding a lean-to village that wasn't worth losing a fly over. Then, alluva sudden, kaboom! This mine goes off and turns Freddy into instant hamburger just like that, and I go flying through the air like a fucking

57

frisbee. The next thing I remember, I wake up in a chopper with a hunka gristle in my sleeve.

The whole damn thing was a no-win war from the start. Fucking Kennedy and Johnson and Nixon—they were outta their minds for sending guys over there. Over fifty-five grand died for those assholes. Over fifty-five grand, Bobby, think of it.

ROSS

Ross pours out his feelings of disdain for a non-feeling parentage.

ROSS

So what! So, the old man is dying? So, what's it have to do with me? You can go on back and wallow and blubber if you want to—not me. I don't want anything to do with the bastards! They're not my family, not the way they treated me. And you? For crisesakes, Jerry, don't you have any pride? They cut off your balls, those people. Hell, they damned near ruined us both. T' hell with the old man.

Where was he when I freaked out and they hauled me off to the mental hospital, huh? He was in Europe somewhere, too busy to come home, too involved with making bucks—that bastard. And Mom? Hell, she didn't give a fuck either. All she was worried about was how me snapping out would make her look in the community, to the face-lifted broads she hangs out with at the club. Hell, nobody raised a finger. *Nobody!* And do you know why? Because they just didn't give a damn!

What in the hell ever happened to caring, Jer? Whatever happened to caring and decency and love and putting your flesh and blood before business and clubs and social horseshit? What ever happened to all that? Is this what it's all about here? That we were born to be rich fucking orphans? Is this it, Jerry? Is it? Or don't you care? Maybe you've gotten like the rest of them. Maybe you hung around too long. Maybe they got to you, too. Maybe some of their indifference rubbed off. Christ, I hope not.

So, he dies, so what! I don't have any feeling about it. He can die without me. He lived without me, now he can die the same way. He's a poor, sorry, rich sonofabitch. All of 'em are! They may have it in the bank, but they'll never have it where it really counts—in the heart.

You go on back if you want. Go on back and grovel and wear your best suit and stand around and get the piss kicked out of your self-esteem. Not me, Jerry! No way!

DANNY

A college student has had it with PC.

DANNY

It's gotten to the point where you can't say a god-damned thing. Everybody's gotten so fucking over-protective of their little hunk of turf, you know. I mean, the attitude of sensitivity out there is ridicu-lous. You've got to go around treading on eggshells. Shit, it seems like everybody has this ax to grind. They're all up to their sensitive little tushes in the po-litical-correctness thing. I mean, Christ—I can't even write an honest criticism anymore.

Like when I said that that fucking off-the-wall dance production they staged last week had all the grace of dogs in heat, you'd thought I'd crapped in the instructor's leotards, or something. He went ballistic. Tried to get me kicked off the paper. He said I showed gross insensitivity. Hey, all I did was write the best review I could based on my experience and knowledge of theater and dance, that's all. And why do I have to be sensitive to a bunch of undisciplined jerks gyrating without form, or structure. Maybe the guy was outraged because I called attention to the fact he's given up teaching basics in favor of inane self-indulgence.

It's like the poetry they submit to us for publication. It's crap. Abstract crap they try to pass off as art; rambling, word-association babble that's supposed to be this, this *profound* social statement. I call it the *Ode to a Texaco Restroom School.* Ginsberg, Ferlinghetti, and the old North Beach crowd can rest easy. Those people were true artists who studied their craft—and worked.

This school's become nothing but a haven for the three M's: the maladjusted, the maladroit, and the malcontent. And because of it, we're graduating a bunch of airheads because everyone's too busy being offended to get an education. We've degenerated into an institution of politically correct bullshit. We've got student-action committees, student-defense councils, student-grievance bodies up the ass. And they're supported by faculty: guys who are so politically biased the patterns in their tweed jackets all run to the left.

I don't know how much longer I'll be able to stay on the paper. I'm getting heat from all directions. I guess my tenure boils down to one, simple, galling fact: I can be entertainment editor as long as I avoid the truth.

FRED

*Fred's weekend outings with girlfriend Lynda are
leading to financial ruin. Here he describes a trip.*

FRED

Forget it. I've got to cool it for a while. I'm broke. I
spent a bundle on Lynda this weekend. A fucking
fortune. I took her to a ballgame, then to dinner at
some nouvelle-cuisine joint she loves where they get
eighty bucks for strained food. But what the hell can
you do? I mean, Lynda's not the kind of woman you
sit around the house with, you know. She wants to do
things and be entertained and go places.

Like here a couple of weeks ago she insists we go
to this bed-and-breakfast place way the hell out in the
boonies. So—off we go. It was like checking into
somebody's house, or something. It was weird. At
first, to be honest, I was pissed. I mean, like, who
wants to live with some strange family and pay for it?
Hell, we could have spent the weekend with my uncle
Carmine for nothing. But once we got settled in, I
gotta admit, it wasn't too bad. It was quaint, you
know.

You should have seen the people who ran the
joint. They were real cute and had faces like polished

63

apples and looked like they'd been carved outta wood in the Black Forest. Hummel dolls. Lynda loved 'em. Especially the old man. She said I should take a lesson from him. How he didn't swear and didn't have to use profanity to make a point. I have to admit, the old guy was a real genteel motherfucker.

The place had only one bathroom for three couples. What a crock. I mean, we could have checked into a nice motel and had a john all to ourselves. But Lynda said that this was part of the charm of the place. Although I can't say I found standing in line with a bunch of dorks in the hallway very charming. But the breakfasts were great, I gotta give 'em that. Biscuits with gravy, and waffles with real maple syrup, and all kinds of homemade jams and jellies. Lynda insisted I buy a couple cases of their orange marmalade. Those bastards weren't quaint when it came to price, I'll tell you that, pal.

The breakfast was great, but the bed was terrible. It had a soft, lumpy mattress, and we kept rolling toward the middle all night long. And the worst part was, we couldn't make it because the springs squeaked, and Lynda said that other people would hear us and it would be embarrassing. Jesus! Forty bucks worth of marmalade and I didn't even get laid.

SAM

Sam bemoans the tragedy of baldness.

SAM

Look, I don't wanna hear about it, okay? Anyway, with the ton of hair you've got, how would you know? It's always you guys with the mop of hair who give all the stupid advice.

You've got no idea what it's like to lose your hair. It affects you and makes you crazy. And all of the silly remarks about not being able to have hair and brains, too, and how bald is beautiful—that doesn't make it any easier. Look, if I had my choice, I'd trade what brains I have for a couple pounds of protein-rich, thick, wavy hair any day.

And all of the rationalizing in the world doesn't help, either. What it comes down to is most women don't go for chrome-domes. All this stuff about how baldness means virility and how the ladies gravitate toward bald-headed men is the biggest scam since Nehru suits. Women don't dig baldies. Period! Not unless the guy's a millionaire. Then it's strictly for the bucks. You take away the money, they're outta there.

And there's nothing you can do about it, either. I know, because I've tried everything. Forget it. And transplants cost a fortune and usually come in strange and you wind up looking like a Chia Pet. And toupees are a joke. They never comb in right and they sit on your head like a dead muskrat. And the weave jobs and clip-ons and all that look awful, too; phony and lifeless and always a shade off in color. Like the stupid piece on the news guy on Channel 6. The sonofabitch looks like he's sitting under a bird's nest.

Frank, there's nothing redeeming about baldness—*nothing!* Thank your lucky fucking stars you look like Godzilla.

JOE

Joe, due to drunken recklessness, is responsible for the death of the woman he loved. In this speech, he reflects contrition and also expresses bitterness for events that he feels contributed to the tragic incident.

JOE

I shoulda known better than t' go over there that day. People should always know when what they do is stupid and wasteful. But sometimes we don't, do we? Nope, sometimes, even when we know there's not a damn bit of sense to it, we go too far. I guess that's just the way it is with us creatures.

And I'd been drinkin' all that morning. Somethin' I should never do. 'Specially when things are wearin' on me. 'Cause liquor at a time like that is somethin' a guy like me hides behind and uses as an excuse to do what he knows he shouldn't. (*beat*)

Yeah, I shoulda stayed away for sure. Maybe it's 'cause Cyrus told me I couldn't come, maybe that's the reason. There ain't nothin' like takin' a thing away from a person to make him want it all the more.

I loved Martha an' just couldn't stand the thought of never seein' 'er again. When the old man said I couldn't, I went crazy; all fuzzy an' outta control;

rollin' downhill without any brakes on me. Joe Ives just wasn't good enough for his daughter. I was good enough for a friend, to work for 'im, but someone like *me* wasn't good enough for his flesh and blood.

He had no right t' try an' keep us apart. No right, goddamnit! So, I just couldn't stay away. I just couldn't help myself, that's all. I've never ever felt so much hurt. Inside I was empty, like someone had turned me over and poured me out. I was sick and angry and in love. In love with the only thing in the world that meant a damn to me, something that alluva sudden I had taken away. And ya know why? 'Cause I wasn't good enough: 'cause I hadn't gone to the right schools—'cause I didn't measure up—'cause I was "different." Hell, alluva sudden I wasn't part of the human race. I was nothin' but a *thing*. But a thing with feelings—that's what he forgot.

DEWEY

Dewey, a hard-knocking, self-made man, speaks with great fervor against the environmental restrictions placed upon industry and of their often-devastating effects.

DEWEY

The point is, this town's been healthy for years becausea Barnes' Manufacturing! This little snot-pile of a burg owes its existence to it! So, we cut a corner here and there. Big fucking deal. Who the hell doesn't?

Nobody ever gave a good goddamn about a little waste being dumped here and there. Not till we got a handful of so-called enlightened people in this county who didn't know shit from Shinola and made a big deal and stuck their noses in and make it damn near impossible for us to operate! Sure, I could have installed the cleanup crap, sure. And it woulda cost a fortune and woulda put a plant the size of mine right outta business! I wonder how half the town woulda felt about being out of work?

Nobody complained except a few liberal, politically correct, self-righteous sonsabitches anyway. Nobody. The local merchants? Are you kidding? The city council? Never! They all knew if we had to meet all of the stupid requirements, we'd be finished and so would they. And they were right. Right because they know the world keeps turning and that they have to get up in the morning and make a living and face the hard realities. And you can't please everybody and bend over backwards and give in to every god-damn stupid whim.

All of this purity crap's for the textbooks. For assholes like you, Brad, who think life's a white shirt that never gets mussed! If it wasn't for guys like me, guys who busted their balls and started on shoestrings and worked and sweated and stayed with it, it would all come to a grinding halt. You may question my ethics—okay, fine. That's your privilege.

I'll tell ya what—you go out and take a vote. Go out and ask the people of this town if they want ethics or wanna eat! Go on, ask 'em—college boy.

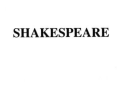

SHAKESPEARE

The Merry Wives of Windsor

Act II. Scene ii. Master Ford, absurdly jealous of his wife, approached Falstaff in the guise of a certain "Master Brook," and commissioned the fat knight to woo Mistress Ford on Brook's behalf. Ford wants proof of Falstaff's conquest of his wife so he can use it to break down her resistance to him in his own wooing of her. Here Ford speaks of the arrangement as a stroke of genius. He also anguishes and vows revenge.

FORD

What a damned Epicuran rascal is this! My heart is ready to crack with impatience. Who says this is improvident jealousy? my wife hath sent to him, the hour is fixed, the match is made. Would any man have thought this? See the hell of having a false woman! My bed shall be abused, my coffers ransacked, my reputation gnawn at; and I shall not only receive this villanous wrong, but stand under the adoption of abominable terms, and by him that does me this wrong. Terms! names! Amaimon sounds well; Lucifer, well; Barbason, well; yet they are devil's additions, the names of friends: but cuckold!

Wittol!—Cuckold! the devil himself hath not such a name. Page is an ass, a secure ass: he will trust his wife; he will not be jealous. I will rather trust a Fleming with my butter, Parson Hugh the Welshman with my cheese, and Irishman with my aquavitae bottle, or a thief to walk my ambling gelding, than my wife with herself: then she plots, then she ruminates, then she devises; and what they think in their hearts they may effect, they will break their hearts but they will effect. God be praised for my jealousy! Eleven o'clock the hour. I will prevent this, detect my wife, be revenged of Falstaff, and laugh at Page. I will about it; better three hours too soon than a minute too late. Fie, fie, fie! Cuckold! cuckold! cuckold!

(Exit)

As You Like It

Act II. Scene vii. Jaques, a lord attending the banished Duke, speaks of the seven ages of man.

JAQUES

                All the world's stage,
And all the men and women merely players:
They have their exits and their entrances;
And one man in his time plays many parts,
His acts being seven ages. At the first the infant,
Mewling and puking in the nurse's arms:
Then the whining school-boy, with his satchel
And shining morning face, creeping like snail
Unwillingly to school: and then the lover,
Sighing like furnace, with a woeful ballad
Made to his mistress' eyebrow: then the soldier,
Full of strange oaths and bearded like a pard,
Jealous in honor, sudden and quick in quarrel,
Seeking the bubble reputation
Even in the cannon's mouth: and then the justice
In fair round belly with good capon lined,
With eyes severe and beard of formal cut,
Full of wise saws and modern instances;
And so he plays his part: the sixth age shifts

Into the lean and slipper'd pantaloon,
With spectacle on nose and pouch on side,
His youthful hose, well saved, a world too wide
For his shrunk shank; and his big manly voice,
Turning again toward childish treble, pipes
And whistles in his sound: last scene of all,
That ends this strange eventful history,
Is second childishness and mere oblivion,
Sans teeth, sans eyes, sans taste, sans everything.

*Act II. Scene i. Stirred by the witches prophecies and
goaded by Lady Macbeth, Macbeth contemplates his
evil deed and awaits the signal that will dispatch him
to the murder of Duncan.*

MACBETH

Is this the dagger which I see before me,
The handle toward my hand? Come, let me clutch
thee.
I have thee not, and yet I see thee still.
Art thou not, fatal vision, sensible
To feeling as to sight? or art thou but
A dagger of the mind, a false creation,
Proceeding from the heat-oppressèd brain?
I see thee yet, in form as palpable
As this which I now draw.
Thou marshallest me the way I was going;
And such an instrument I was to use.
Mine eyes are made the fools o' the other senses,
Or else worth all the rest; I see thee still,
And on my blade and dudgeon gouts of blood,
Which was not so before. There's no such thing:
It is the bloody business which informs

Thus to mine eyes. Now o'er the one half-world
Nature seems dead, and wicked dreams abuse
The curtained sleep; witchcraft celebrates
Pale Hecate's offerings, and withered murder,
Alarumed by his sentinel, the wolf,
Whose howl's his watch, thus with his stealthy pace,
With Tarquin's ravishing strides, towards his design
Moves like a ghost. Thou sure and firm-set earth,
Hear not my steps, which may they walk, for fear
Thy very stones prate of my whereabout,
And take the present horror from the time,
Which now suits with it. Whiles I threat, he lives:
Words to heat of deeds to cold breath gives.

    (*a bell rings*)

I go, and it is done; the bell invites me.
Here it not, Duncan; for it is a knell
That summons the to heaven or to hell.

    (*Exit*)

Othello

Act II. Scene ii: The duplicitous Iago contrives to set Othello the Moor against his lieutenant Cassio and instill jealousy in him for his wife Desdemona. He instigates a drunken brawl involving Cassio and then summons Othello to investigate. After Othello finds his lieutenant derelict of duties and discharges him, Iago encourages Cassio to ask for Desdemona's help in restoring him to his position of authority and regaining Othello's confidence. Iago's motive here is to make Othello believe that she is pleading Cassio's case out of her love for him.

IAGO

And what's he then that says I play the villain,
When this advice is free I give and honest,
Probal to thinking, and indeed the course
To win the Moor again? For 'tis most easy
The inclining Desdemona to subdue
In any honest suit. She's fram'd as fruitful
As the free elements. And then for her
To win the Moor—were't to renounce his baptism—
All seals and symbols of redeemed sin,
His soul is so enfetter'd to her love,

That she may make, unmake, do what she list,
Even as her appetite shall play the god
With his weak function. How am I then a villain
To counsel Cassio to this parallel course,
Directly to his good? Divinity of hell!
When devils will the blackest sins put on,
They do suggest at first with heavenly shows,
As I do now: for whiles this honest fool
Plies Desdemona to repair his fortunes,
And she for him pleads strongly to the Moor,
I'll pour this pestilence into his ear—
That she repeals him for her body's lust;
And by how much she strives to do him good,
She shall undo her credit with the Moor.
So I will turn her virtue into pitch,
And out of her own goodness make the net
That shall enmesh them all.

Julius Caesar

Act III. Scene i. First, in the presence of Caesar's murderers, Mark Antony feigns understanding and embraces them, appearing to make peace.

ANTONY

                 I doubt not of your wisdom,
Let each man render me his bloody hand.
First, Marcus Brutus, will I shake with you;
Next, Caius Cassius, do I take your hand;
Now, Decius Brutus, yours; now yours, Metellus;
Yours, Cinna; and, my valiant Casca, yours.
Though last, not least in love, yours, good Trebonius.
Gentlemen all, alas—what shall I say?
My credit now stands on such slippery ground,
That one of two bad ways you must conceit me,
Either a coward or a flatterer.
That I did love thee, Caesar, O, 'tis true:
If then thy spirit look upon us now,
Shall it now grieve thee dearer than thy death
To see thy Antony making his peace,
Shaking the bloody fingers of thy foes,
Most noble! in the presence of thy corse?
Had I as many eyes as thou hast wounds,

Weeping as fast as they stream forth thy blood,
It would become me better than to close
In terms of friendship with thine enemies.
Pardon me, Julius!   Here wast thou bayed, brave
heart;
Here didst thou fall; and here my hunters stand,
Signed in thy spoil, and crimson'd in they lethe.
O world, thou wast the forest to this heart;
And this indeed, O world, the heart of thee!
How like a deer, stroken by many princes,
Dost thou here lie!

CHEKOV, WILDE, SHAW

Anton Chekov

The Seagull

Act Four. Treplev. A drawing room in the Sorin estate.

Two years earlier, Nina ran off with the famous writer Trigorin, who proved to be a spineless roué. Here, Treplev updates Dr. Dorn relative to her adventures, and exposes his enduring attachment to his beloved Nina.

TREPLEV

Of course, you know she ran away with Trigorin. And had his baby and the baby died. Then Trigorin got tired of her and went back to his old attachments, as you might expect. In fact, he'd never given them up. He'd been looking back and forth between Nina and his old loves in keeping with his weak character. From what I've heard, Nina's life has been a disaster. Her stage career even worse, it seems. She made her debut at a little resort near Moscow, then went on a tour of the provinces. I never let her out of my sight in those days, and wherever she appeared, I followed.

She tried to play all the big parts, but her acting was crude and tasteless and full of ranting and stiff gestures. Oh, there were moments, of course. Every now and then she cried well, sometimes her dying scenes were effective. She had some talent, I suppose, but it was hard to tell. I saw her, but she wouldn't see me. Her maid wouldn't let me into her room. I knew how she felt, so I didn't push it. (*pause*) What else can I tell you? After I came home, I got some letters from her that were warm, intelligent, and provocative, and she didn't complain. But I could tell she was very unhappy because there was tension in every line. You could tell she was upset. She kept signing her letters "The Seagull." And she kept referring to herself as a seagull, like the miller in *The Mermaid* kept calling himself a raven. She's here now, you know? In town, at the inn. She's been here for about five days. I've tried to see her, and Masha has tried, too. But she won't see anyone.

Anton Chekov

Uncle Vanya

Act One. Voynitsky. A garden on the Serebryakov estate.

Professor Serebryakov's return to the estate with his young bride, Elena, has caused Uncle Vanya (Voynitsky) to lose interest in managing the property. He has come to see through the professor and now views him as an untalented, arrogant, complaining bore. Here he voices his feelings and—with thinly veiled jealously due to the fact he is smitten with Elena—marvels at Serebryakov's success with women.

VOYNITSKY

I've nothing new to tell. It's the same old story. I'm still the same, except maybe worse because I've become lazy and don't do anything but fret around like a grouch. And my mother sits around raving about the emancipation of women. She's got one eye on the grave and one in her books of learning for a way to a new life. And the professor, like always, sits in his study, writing from morning till night.

> "With furrowed brow and toiling brain
> We write our epic odes,
> But neither we nor they will ever hear
> A bit of praise no matter what we write."

I feel sorry for the paper he writes on. He'd be better off writing his autobiography. Oh, what a subject that would be. A retired professor, get it, this dried up old mackerel with gout, rheumatism, and migraine with a liver swollen with jealously and envy—this well-educated, smoked fish living on his first wife's estate against his will because he hasn't got the money to live in town.

He's always endlessly complaining about his misfortunes, although, in fact, he's damned lucky. (*Nervously.*) How lucky can you get? He's nothing but the son of a common sexton, educated at a church school. He picked up degrees at a university and got a professorship and became this important person because he married a senator's daughter. All of this really doesn't mean anything, but just the same . . . here we have a person who for twenty-five years has lectured and written about art and who doesn't know a thing about it. For twenty-five years he's been writing and lecturing what intelligent people have known for years and what stupid people have no interest in. To be blunt, for twenty-five years he's been pouring from one empty pot to another. And at the same time what monumental conceit! What arrogance! What pretensions! Here he is retired and not one single living soul knows who he is. He's a complete unknown! For twenty-five years the man has been working in someone else's place. And look at him. He stalks around like a demigod! And I envy him! He's such a success with women! No Don Juan has ever done better! My own sister, his first wife, a beautiful, gentle woman, pure as the blue sky, noble and generous, who had more admirers than he had students—she loved him as only angels can love those who are as pure and beautiful as they. And my own mother, his mother-in-law, she still worships him with reverent awe. And his second wife, beautiful, intelligent—you just saw her—married him when he was already old and gave him her youth, her beauty, her freedom, her special radiance. And for what? Why?

Anton Chekov

The Cherry Orchard

Act Two. Trofimov. A field.

Trofimov, a student, speaks of the folly of man's pride, the ignorance of Russia's so-called intelligentsia, inhuman realities abounding in his homeland.

TROFIMOV

We talked a lot yesterday and didn't settle a thing. When you talk about man's pride, you're referring to the mystical, spiritual side of him. Maybe from that point of view, you're right . . . maybe. But if you sort out the whole thing without emotion, look at it clearly, then what's to be proud of when you realize what a poor psychological specimen man is and how most of the human race is brutal, stupid, and profoundly unhappy? It's high time we stop admiring ourselves. The only thing to do is work. Humanity marches on, perfecting itself. All the things that are incomprehensible to us now will one day be commonplace if we apply ourselves and work and do all we can for those who seek the truth.

Today in Russia, very few people really work. All the educated people I know—most of them, anyway—are lazy and passive. They don't know what it is to work. They have the nerve to call themselves the intelligentsia while they talk down to their servants and treat the peasants like animals. Some students! They're lazy, they read pap, talk about science, and when it comes to art—they don't know a damned thing about it. These "serious" little people with grim faces. While they discuss and philosophize, right under their noses the workers are poorly fed, sleep in filthy bedding, thirty or forty to a room with bedbugs everywhere and foul odors and dampness and moral corruption!

Clearly, all of our high-minded talk is just a way of deceiving ourselves and others. Tell me—where are all the nurseries they're always talking about? Where are the libraries? They're aren't any. They only exist in their vacuous little novels. What does exist is filth and ugliness and barbarity. I hate these grim faces and serious conversations—they frighten me. We'd all be better off if we'd just keep our mouths shut for a while.

Anton Chekov

The Three Sisters

Act Three. Andrei. The garden of the Prozorov house.

Andrei, the sisters' brother, was once an energetic man striving for a professional future. However, he has fallen under the influence of his crude, conniving wife, Natasha, and has taken a position on the City Council, a position arranged for him by his wife's lover, Protopopov. Now nothing more than a lethargic pawn, he bemoans his life, is repulsed by the inhabitants of the city, whom he views as evolving generations of slothful, decadent individuals.

ANDREI

Oh where is my past life, where did it go—when I was young and happy and intelligent, when I had great dreams and could think and my present and future were bright and hopeful? Why do we become dull and useless and unhappy just when we've barely started to live? Here's a town two hundred years old with over a hundred thousand people who are all exactly alike. There's never been one saint, one scholar, one artist, not a single person out of the ordinary whom anyone would want to emulate. All these people do is eat and drink and sleep, and—to beat boredom, to put a little spice in their lives—they gossip and drink and play cards and bring lawsuits. And wives deceive their husbands, and husbands keep on lying and pretend to see and hear nothing. And the children are oppressed by their parents' shallow and trivial lives, and all hope is killed in them, and—just like their fathers and mothers before them—they become tragic corpses, one identical to the other.

Oscar Wilde

Vera; or, The Nihilists

Act II

Ivan the Czar declares war on the Nihilists who are threatening revolution.

CZAR

For two years her hands have been clutching at my throat; for two years she has made my life hell; but I shall have revenge. Martial law, Prince, martial law over the whole Empire; that will give me revenge. A good measure, Prince, eh? A good measure.

(*standing*) I am sick of being afraid. I have done with terror now. From this day I proclaim war against the people—war to their annihilation. As they have dealt with me, so shall I deal with them. I shall grind them to powder, and strew their dust upon the air. There shall be a spy in every man's house, a traitor on every hearth, a hangman in every village, a gibbet in every square. Plague, leprosy, or fever shall be less deadly than my wrath; I will make every frontier a graveyard, every province a lazar-house, and cure the sick by the sword. I shall have peace in Russia, though it be the peace of the dead. Who said I was coward? Who said I was afraid? See, thus shall I crush this people beneath my feet? (*takes the sword from the table and tramples it*)

Oscar Wilde

The Importance of Being Earnest,

Act III

Jack refuses to give his permission to his ward, Cecily Cardew, to marry Algernon. In this speech, he explains his reasons for his decision.

JACK

I beg your pardon for interrupting you, Lady Bracknell, but this engagement is quite out of the question. I am Miss Cardew's guardian, and she cannot marry without my consent until she comes of age. That consent I absolutely decline to give.

It pains me very much to have to speak frankly to you, Lady Bracknell, about your nephew, but the fact is that I do not approve at all of his moral character. I suspect him of being untruthful.

I fear there can be no possible doubt about the matter. This afternoon during my temporary absence in London on an important question of romance, he obtained admission to my house by means of the false pretense of being my brother. Under an assumed name he drank, I've just been informed by my butler, an entire pint bottle of my Perrier-Jouet, Brut '89, a wine I was specially reserving for myself. Continuing his disgraceful deception, he succeeded in the course of the afternoon in alienating the affections of my only ward. He subsequently stayed to tea, and devoured every single muffin. And what makes his conduct all the more heartless is that he was perfectly aware from the first that I have no brother, that I never had a brother, and that I don't intend to have a brother, not even of any kind. I distinctly told him so myself yesterday afternoon.

Oscar Wilde

Lady Windermere's Fan

Act II

Lord Darlington reveals his love to Lady Windermere.

LORD DARLINGTON

If I know you at all, I know that you can't live with a man who treats you like this! What sort of life would you have with him? You would feel that he was lying to you every moment of the day. You would feel that the look in his eyes was false, his voice false, his touch false, his passion false. He would come to you when he was weary of others; you would have to comfort him. He would come to you when he was devoted to others; you would have to charm him. You would have to be to him the mask of his real life, the cloak to hide his secret.

Between men and women there is no friendship possible. There is passion, enmity, worship, love, but no friendship. I love you—

Yes, I love you! You are more to me than anything in the whole world. What does your husband give you? Nothing. Whatever is in him he gives to this wretched woman, whom he has thrust into your society, into your home, to shame you before everyone. I offer you my life —

My life—my whole life. Take it, do with it what you will—I love you—love you as I have never loved any living thing. From the moment I met you I loved you, loved you blindly, adoringly, madly! You did not know it then—you know it now! Leave this house tonight. I won't tell you that the world matters nothing, or the world's voice, or the voice of society. They matter a great deal. They matter far too much. But there are moments when one has to choose between living one's own life, full, entirely, completely—or dragging out some false, shallow, degrading existence that the world in its hypocrisy demands. You have that moment now. Choose! Oh, my love, choose! You have the courage.

There may be six months of pain, of disgrace even, but when you no longer bear his name, when you bear mine, all will be well. Margaret, my love, my wife that shall be someday—yes, my wife! You know it! What are you now? This woman has the place that belongs by right to you. Oh, go—go out of this house, with head erect, with a smile upon your lips, with courage in your eyes. All London will know why you did it; and who will blame you? No One. If they do, what matter? Wrong? What is wrong? It's wrong for a man to abandon his wife for a shameless woman. It is wrong for a wife to remain with a man who so dishonors her. You said once you would make no compromise with things. Make none now. Be brave! Be yourself!

Oscar Wilde

Salome

Herod attempts to talk Salome out of her demands for the head of John the Baptist.

HEROD

Silence! Do not speak to me. Look here, Salome, be sensible. We must be sensible, you know. I have never been harsh with you. I have always loved you. Perhaps I have loved you too much. So do not ask that of me. That request is horrible, frightful. I cannot believe you mean it seriously. A man's decapitated head is an ugly thing, do you not realize? Not a thing for a virgin to look at. What possible pleasure could it afford you? None. No, no, you would not wish for that—Listen to me a moment. I have an emerald, a great round emerald that Caesar's favorite sent to me. Look into it and you can see things that are happening far away. Caesar himself wears an emerald like it when he goes to the circus. But mine is larger. It is the largest emerald in the world. Surely that is what you would like to have? Ask me for it and I will give it to you.

Salome, you know those white peacocks of mine, those marvelous white peacocks that walk about the garden between the myrtles and the tall cypresses? Their beaks are gilded, and the grains they eat are gilded too, and their feet are stained with purple. When they cry out the rain comes, and when they spread their tails the moon appears in the sky. They move two-by-two among the cypresses and the black myrtles and each has a slave to care for it. Sometimes they fly atop the trees and sometimes they crouch in the grass and beside the pool. The world cannot show any birds so marvelous as these. No king in the world possesses such birds. I am sure that even Caesar has no birds so beautiful. Well, then, I will give you fifty of my peacocks. They will follow you everywhere, and in the midst of them you will be like the moon surrounded by a great white cloud . . . I will give you all of them. Only, you must release me from my oath and not ask me for what you have asked.

Oscar Wilde

The Duchess of Padua

Act III

After not kill ing the Duke, Guido prays to God, ex-
plaining his actions, and giving further explanation
regarding the letter that he plans to leave for the
Duke, telling that he had spared his life.

GUIDO

Thou, father, knowest of my intent and art content
with this nobler vengeance. Whenas I grant the man
his life, I ween I am doing as thou would'st have
done thyself. I cannot tell, father, whether human
voice can break through the iron prison of the dead,
whether the departed have any tidings of what we do
and leave undone for their sakes. And yet, methinks, I
feel a presence near me, like a shadow by my side,
and meseems as though spirit kisses touched my lips
and left them sanctified. (*he kneels*) Oh father, canst
thou not break the laws of Death and show thyself in
bodily shape, that I may grasp thy hand? Nay, nay,
'tis naught. (*rises*) It is the midnight phantoms do

befool us, the night deceives us like a puppet-show-man, persuading us that what is not, is. 'Tis waxing late; I must now to my work. (*he pulls a letter from his bosom and reads*) When he awakes and sees this letter and dagger beside it, disgust will take hold of him for his life. Will he mayhap repent and reform his ways? Or will he mock, because a young wight hath spared him, his bitter enemy? 'Tis all one to me. Thy errand, father, it is that I fulfill—thy orders and my love's, which hath taught me to know thee as thou art.

G. B. Shaw

Man and Superman

Act I

John Tanner is telling Octavius, a self-proclaimed artist and sensitive human being, what the true characteristics of an
artist are.

TANNER

The true artist will let his wife starve, his children go barefoot, his mother drudge for his living at seventy, sooner than work at anything but his art. To women he is half vivisector, half vampire. He gets into intimate relations with them to study them, to strip the mask of convention from them, to surprise their in-innermost secrets, knowing that they have the power to rouse his deepest creative energies, to rescue him from his cold reason, to make him see visions and dream dreams, to inspire him, as he calls it. He persuades women that they may do this for their own purpose whilst he really means them to do it for his. He steals the mother's milk and blackens it to make printer's ink to scoff at her and glorify ideal women with. He pretends to spare her the pangs of child-bearing so that he may have for himself the tenderness and fostering that belong of right to her children. Since marriage began, the great artist has been known as a bad husband. But he is worse: He is a child-robber, a blood-sucker, a hypocrite and a cheat. Perish the race and wither a thousand women if only the sacrifice of them enable him to act Hamlet better, to paint a finer picture, to write a deeper poem, a greater play, a profounder philosophy! For mark you, Tavy, the artist's work is to shew us ourselves as we really are. Our minds are nothing but this knowledge of ourselves; and he who adds a jot to such knowledge creates new mind as surely as any woman creates new men. In the rage of that creation he is as ruthless as the women, as dangerous to her as she to him, and as horribly fascinating. Of all human struggles there is none so treacherous and remorseless as the struggle between the artist man and the mother woman. Which shall use up the other? that is the issue between them. And it is all the deadlier because, in your romanticist cant, they love one another.

G. B. Shaw

The Doctor's Dilemma

Act I

Ridgeon describes the discovery that got him knighted.

RIDGEON

No: It's not gammon. What it comes to in practice is this. The phagocytes won't eat the microbes unless the microbes are nicely buttered for them. Well, the patient manufactures the butter for himself all right; but my discovery is that the manufacture of that butter, which I call opsonin, goes on in the system by ups and downs—Nature being always rhythmical, you know—and that what the inoculation does is to stimulate the ups and downs, as the case may be. If we had inoculated Jane Marsh when her butter factory was on the up-grade, we should have cured her arm. But we got in on the down-grade and lost her arm for her. I call the up-grade the positive phase and the down-grade the negative phase. Everything depends on your inoculating at the right moment.

Inoculate when the patient is in the negative phase and you kill: Inoculate when the patient is in the positive phase and you cure. Send a drop of the patient's blood to the laboratory at St. Anne's, and in fifteen minutes I'll give you his opsonin index in figures. If the figure is one, inoculate and cure: If it's under point eight, inoculate and kill. That's my discovery: The most important that has been made since Harvey discovered the circulation of the blood. My tuberculosis patients don't die now.

G. B. Shaw

Captain Brassbound's Conversion

Act III

Captain Brassbound, who has scorned love in the past, proposes marriage to Lady Cicely.

BRASSBOUND

I want a commander. Don't undervalue me: I am a good man when I have a good leader. I have courage: I have determination: I'm not a drinker: I can command a schooner and a shore party if I can't command a ship or an army. When work is put upon me, I turn neither to save my life nor to fill my pocket. Gordon trusted me: and he never regretted it. If you trust me, you shant regret it. All the same, there's something wanting in me: I suppose I'm stupid. Since you saw me for the first time in that garden, you've heard me say nothing clever. And I've heard you say nothing that didn't make me laugh, or make me feel friendly, as well as telling me what to think and what to do. That's what I mean by real cleverness. Well, I haven't got it.

I can give an order when I know what order to give. I can make men obey it, willing or unwilling. But I'm stupid, I tell you: Stupid. When there's no Gordon to command me, I can't think of what to do. Left to myself, I've become half a brigand. I can kick that little gutterscrub Drinkwater; but I find myself doing what he puts into my head because I can't think of anything else.

When you came, I took your orders as naturally as Gordon's, though I little thought my next commander would be a woman. I want to take service under you. And there is no way in which that can be done except marrying you. Will you let me do it?

G. B. Shaw

You Never Can Tell

Act II

*A waiter gives a truer philosophy of life than any of
the upper classes is capable of giving.*

WAITER

(*philosophically*) Well, sir, you never can tell. That's
the principle in life with me, sir, if you'll excuse my
having such a thing, sir. (*artfully loosing the philoso-
pher for a moment*) Perhaps you haven't noticed that
you hadn't touched that seltzer and Irish, sir, when
the party broke up. (*sets a tumbler before Crampton*)
Yes, sir, you never can tell. There was my son, sir!
whoever thought that he would rise to wear a silk
gown, sir? What a lesson, sir. (*artfully digressing*) A
lump of sugar, sir, will take the flatness out of the
seltzer without noticeably sweetening the drink, sir.
Allow me, sir. (*places the tumbler*) But as I say to
him, where's the difference after all? If I must put on
a dress coat to show what I am, sir, he must put on a
wig and gown to show what he is. If my income is

111

mostly tips, and there's a pretense that I don't get them, why, his income is mostly fees, sir; and I understand that there's a pretense that he don't get them! If he likes society, and if his profession brings him into contact with all ranks, so does mine too, sir. If it's a little against a barrister to have a waiter for his father, sir, it's a little against a waiter to have a barrister for a son; many people consider it a great liberty, sir, I assure you, sir. Can I get you anything else, sir?

G. B. Shaw

The Admirable Bashville; or, Constancy Unrewarded

Act II

The servant, Bashville, is reading a newspaper account of a boxing match, in which Cashel Byron (the man Lydia loves) has participated.

BASHVILLE

(*reading*) "At noon today, unknown to
the police,
Within a thousand miles of Wormwood Scrubbs,
The Australian Champion and his challenger,
The Flying Dutchman, formerly engaged
I' the mercantile marine, fought to a finish.
Lord Worthington, the well-known sporting peer,
Was early on the scene."

       "The bold Ned Skene revisited the ropes
To hold the bottle for his quondam novice;
Whilst in the seaman's corner were assembled
Professor Palmer and the Chelsea Snob.
Mellish, whose epigastrium has been hurt,

Tis said, by accident at Wiltstoken,
Looked none the worse in the Australian's corner.
The Flying Dutchman wore the Union Jack:
His colors freely sold amid the crowd;
But Cashel's well-known spot of white on blue—
Was fairly rushed for. Time was called at twelve,
When, with a smile of confidence upon
His ocean-beaten mug— "

      "The Dutchman came undaunted to
the scratch,
But found the champion there already. Both
Most heartily shook hands, amid the cheers
Of their encouraged backers. Two to one
Was offered on the Melbourne nonpareil;
And soon, so fit the Flying Dutchman seemed,
Found takers everywhere. No time was lost
In getting to the business of the day.
The Dutchman led at once, and seemed to land
On Byron's dicebox; but the seaman's reach,
Too short for execution at long shots,
Did not get fairly home upon the ivory;
And Byron had the best of the exchange."

      "Round Three: the rumors that had
gone about
Of a breakdown in Byron's training
Seemed quite confirmed. Upon the call of time

He rose, and, looking anything but cheerful,
Proclaimed with every breath Bellows to Mend.
At this point six to one was freely offered
Upon the Dutchman; and Lord Worthington
Plunged at this figure till he stood to lose
A fortune should the Dutchman, as seemed certain,
Take down the number of the Panley boy.
The Dutchman, glutton as we know he is,
Seemed this time likely to go hungry. Cashel
Was clearly groggy as he slipped the sailor,
Who, not to be denied, followed him up,
Forcing the fighting mid tremendous cheers."

     "Forty to one, the Dutchman's friends ex-
claimed.
Done, said Lord Worthington, who shewed himself
A sportsman every inch. Barely the bet
Was booked, when, at the reeling champion's jaw
The sailor, bent on winning out of hand,
Sent his right. The issue seemed a cert,
When Cashel, ducking smartly to his left,
Cross-countered like a hundredweight of brick— "

     "A scene of indescribable excitement
Ensued; for it was now quite evident
That Byron's grogginess had all along
Been feigned to make the market of his backers.
We trust this sample of colonial smartness

Will not find imitators on this side.
The losers settled up like gentlemen;
But many thought that Byron shewed bad taste
In taking out old Ned Skene upon his back,
And, with Bob Mellish tucked beneath his oxter,
Sprinting a hundred yards to show the crowd
The perfect pink of his condition."

G. B. Shaw

How He Lied to Her Husband

Her Husband comes upon He and She as they are deciding the best way to continue their love affair.

HER HUSBAND

What is Mrs. Bompas to you, I'd like to know. I'll tell you what Mrs. Bompas is. She's the smartest woman in the smartest set in South Kensington, and the handsomest, and the cleverest, and the most fetching to experienced men who know a good thing when they see it, whatever she may be to conceited penny-a-lining puppies who think nothing good enough for them. It's admitted by the best people; and not to know it argues yourself unknown. Three of our actor-managers have offered her a hundred a week if she'll go on the stage when they start a repertory theater; and I think they know what they're about as well as you. The only member of the present Cabinet that you might call a handsome man has neglected the business of the country to dance with her, though he don't belong to our set as a regular thing. One of the most professional poets in Bedford Park wrote a sonnet to her, worth all your amateur trash. At Ascot last season the eldest son of a duke excused himself from calling on me on the ground that his feelings for Mrs. Bompas were not consistent with his duty to me as a host; and it did him honor and me too.

But (*with gathering fury*)

she isn't good enough for you, it seems. You regard her with coldness, with indifference; and you have the cool cheek to tell me so to my face.

For two pins I'd flatten your nose in to teach you manners. Introducing a fine woman to you is casting pearls before swine (*screaming at him*) before SWINE! d'ye hear?

G. B. Shaw

Arms and the Man

Act I

The Man (Bluntschli) has broken into Petkoff's house after deserting his regiment, and is attempting to explain his contempt for war to Raina.

MAN

There are only two sorts of soldiers: old ones and young ones. I've served fourteen years: half of your fellows never smelt powder before. Why, how is it that you've just beaten us? Sheer ignorance of the art of war, nothing else. (*indignantly*) I never saw anything so unprofessional. Is it professional to throw a regiment of cavalry on a battery of machine guns, with the dead certainty that if the guns go off not a horse or man will ever get within fifty yards of the fire? I couldn't believe my eyes when I saw it. It's a funny sight. It's like slinging a handful of peas against a window pane: First one comes; then two or three close behind him; and then all the rest are in a lump. That's what you'd have said if you'd seen the first man in the charge today. He did it like an operatic tenor—a regular handsome fellow, with flashing eyes and lovely mustache, shouting a war-cry and charging like Don Quixote at windmills. We nearly burst with laughter at him; but when the sergeant ran up as white as a sheet, and told us they'd sent us the wrong cartridges, and that we couldn't fire a shot for the next ten minutes, we laughed at the other side of our mouths. I never felt so sick in my life, though I've been in one or two very tight places. And I hadn't even a revolver cartridge—nothing but chocolate. We'd no bayonets—nothing. Of course, they just cut us to bits. And there was Don Quixote flourishing like a drum major, thinking he'd done the cleverest thing ever known, whereas he ought to be court-martialed for it. Of all the fools ever let loose on the field of battle, that man must be the very maddest. He and his regiment simply committed suicide—only the pistol missed fire, that's all.

G. B. Shaw

Candida

Act I

Morell tries to explain to Marchbanks why a relationship, illicit or otherwise, could never exist between Marchbanks and Morell's wife, Candida.

MORELL

(*he speaks with noble tenderness*) Eugene: Listen to me. Some day, I hope and trust, you will be a happy man like me. You will be married; and you will be working with all your might and valor to make every spot on earth as happy as your own home. You will be one of the makers of the Kingdom of Heaven on earth; and—who knows?—you may be a pioneer and master builder where I am only a humble journeyman; for don't think, my boy, that I cannot see in you, young as you are, a promise of higher powers than I can ever pretend to. I well know that it is in the poet that the holy spirit of man—the god within him—is most godlike. It should make you tremble to think of that—to think that the heavy burthen and great gift of a poet may be laid upon you.

In the future—when you are as happy a I am—I will be your true brother in the faith. I will help you to believe that God has given us a world that nothing but our own folly keeps from being a paradise. I will help you to believe that your wife loves you and is happy in her home.

We need such help, Marchbanks: We need it greatly and always. There are so many things to make us doubt, if once we let our understanding be troubled. Even at home, we sit as if in a camp, encompassed by the hostile army of doubts. Will you play the traitor and let them in on me?